D0292346

LISTENING FOR OUR SONG

LISTENING FOR OUR SONG

Collected Meditations, Volume Four

COLLECTED BY

MARGARET L. BEARD

SKINNER HOUSE BOOKS

BOSTON

Published by Skinner House Books. Skinner House Books is an imprint of the Unitarian Universalist Association, a liberal religious organization with more than 1,000 congregations in the U.S. and Canada. 25 Beacon Street, Boston, MA 02108-2800.

Printed in Canada

ISBN 1-55896-438-x

Library of Congress Cataloging-in-Publication Data

Listening for our song / collected by Margaret L. Beard.
    p.cm. — (Collected meditations ; v. 4)
  ISBN 1-55896-438-X (alk. paper)
    1. Meditations. 2. Spiritual life—Unitarian Universalist churches—Meditations. 3. Unitarian Universalist churches—Prayer-books and devotions—English. I. Beard, Margaret L., 1952- II. Series.

BX9855 .L57 2002
242—dc21   2002030289

5 4 3 2 1
05 04 03 02

The selections included here were previously published by Skinner House Books as follows: *A Small Heaven,* Jane Ranney Rzepka, 1989; *A Temporary State of Grace,* David S. Blanchard, 1997; *Life Tides,* Elizabeth Tarbox, 1993; *Into the Wilderness,* Sara Moores Campbell (now Sarah York), 1990 (now available from The Apollo Ranch Institute Press).

Excerpt from "Little Gidding" in *Four Quartets,* copyright 1942 by T. S. Eliot and renewed 1970 by Esme Valerie Eliot, reprinted by permission of Harcourt, Inc.

TABLE OF CONTENTS

BETWEEN SEASONS

KALEIDOSCOPE

"It is good to know our songs by heart for those lonely times when the world is not singing them back to us," writes David Blanchard in his meditation "Listening for Our Song." We each have our own unique songs that reflect our life experiences and our particular wisdom. We carry the tunes around with us always but sometimes forget the words when the world distracts us with its daily obligations. This collection is designed for such times. Read these meditations in the morning to center yourself, at various points throughout the day to find comfort or inspiration, or in the evening to quiet yourself before sleep. These are the songs of David Blanchard, Elizabeth Tarbox, Sarah York, and Jane Rzepka, but they may also be your songs. In the moments of surprise, gratitude, understanding, and compassion written about here, may you both find new songs and hear the sound of the world singing back to you the music of your heart.

The meditations in this collection have been selected from meditation manuals published by the Unitarian Universalist Association. As such they reflect the theological diversity of Unitarian Universalism, a non-creedal religion that draws inspiration from many faith traditions. Unitarians and Universalists have been publishing annual editions of prayer collections and meditation manuals for more than 150 years. In 1841 the Unitarians broke with their tradition of addressing only theological topics and published *Short Prayers for the Morning and Evening of Every Day in the Week with Occasional Prayers and Thanksgivings*. Over the years, the Unitarians published many volumes of prayers, and in 1938, *Gaining a Radiant Faith* by Henry H. Saunderson launched the tradition of an annual Lenten manual. During the late 1860s, the Universalist Publishing House was founded to publish denominational materials. Like the Unitarians, the Universalists published Lenten Manuals and in the 1950s they complemented this series with Advent manuals. Since 1961, the year the two denominations combined to form the Unitarian Universalist Association, the Lenten manuals evolved into meditation manuals, reflecting the theological diversity of the two denominations.

Enjoy these meditations. In the words of David Blanchard, they are "songs of love or of longing, songs of encouragement or of comfort, songs of struggle or of security. But most of all, they are the songs of life." In them may you hear again your own song.

MARGARET L. BEARD

LISTENING FOR OUR SONG

LISTENING FOR OUR SONG

On sabbatical in East Africa, I heard a story of a people who believe that we are each created with our own song. Their tradition as a community is to honor that song by singing it as welcome when a child is born, as comfort when the child is ill, in celebration when the child marries, and in affirmation and love when death comes. Most of us were not welcomed into the world in that way. Few of us seem to know our song.

It takes a while for many of us to figure out which is our song, and which is the song that others would like us to sing. Some of us are slow learners. I heard my song not necessarily from doing extraordinary things in exotic places, but also from doing some pretty ordinary things in some routine places. For every phrase I heard climbing Kilimanjaro, I learned another in a chair in a therapist's office. For every measure I heard in the silence of a retreat, I heard another laughing with my girls. For every note I heard in the wind on the beach at Lamu, I gleaned more from spending time with a dying friend as her children sang her song back to her. What came to astound me was not that the song appeared, but that it was always there.

I figure that the only way I could have known it for my own was if I had heard it before, before memory went to work making sense and order of the mystery of our beginning. Our songs sing back to us something of our essence, something of our truth, something of our uniqueness. When our songs are sung back to us, it is not about approval, but about recognizing our being and our belonging in the human family.

It is good to know our songs by heart for those lonely times when the world is not singing them back to us. That's usually a good time to start humming to yourself, that song that is most your own.

They can be heard as songs of love or of longing, songs of encouragement or of comfort, songs of struggle or of security. But most of all, they are the songs of life, giving testimony to what has been, giving praise for all we're given, giving hope for all we strive for, giving voice to the great mystery that carries each of us in and out of this world.

DAVID S. BLANCHARD

ALL IS DUKKHA

"All is *dukkha,*" say the Buddhists. I am told that *dukkha* is hard to translate. It means literally "suffering," but the feeling of *dukkha* is closer to impermanence; impermanence is central to the Buddhist path to nirvana, enlightenment.

Dukkha, all is impermanence, nothing lasts. I thought of that yesterday while watching leaves come down in a shower and inhaling the smell of rotting leaves returning to the earth. Leaf to humus and back to the earth to nourish the roots of the mother tree. The crows crying as the leaves fall and their nests are exposed—*dukkha,* all is impermanence.

Life goes by, and people who were with us last year at this time have died. All souls pass on, all is *dukkha,* nothing lasts.

The Buddhist path to enlightenment is understanding, accepting impermanence to the point where we no longer struggle against it. But here in the West we search for that which is permanent even as we live with ceaseless change and uncertainty. We search for a sure footing on the path strewn with fallen leaves; we notice the buds of next year's growth tightly curled and waiting; we hold on to the things we can count on: our church, our community, our memories of those who died before us, our love and hope, and our search for truth in a world that is *dukkha.*

Spirit of creation, Goddess of today—let us find each other in a changing world; let us experience love as something which exists, a possibility which is. Let us know that we are alive and being renewed miraculously each second; that the impermanence gives to life its freshness and surprise; that our

memories of yesterday and our expectations of
tomorrow make now a cherished, precious, eternal
moment.

ELIZABETH TARBOX

THE HEALING MOMENT

Each day I am newly reminded of my unworthiness:
a dozen thoughts misspoken; another day when the
good I do falls so far short of the good that I could
do; myriad small interchanges, moments of sharing
that strain to the breaking point my desire to be
generous, helpful, and kind; months of careful work
lost by a moment's impatience, a careless word.

But when I am here at the edge of creation,
breaking with the small tide over the sand, the need
to do good rolls away; the question of what is right
diminishes to insignificance and is easily borne away
by the tiny waves. Here, where no words are spoken,
none are misspoken.

I am with the broken stubble of the marsh grass
that holds on through the wrecking wind and the
burning flood. I am with the grains that mold
themselves around everything, accepting even so
unworthy a foot as mine, holding and shaping it
until it feels that it belongs. I stand somewhere

between truth and vision, and what I don't know ceases to embarrass me, because what I do know is that the water feels gentle like a lover's touch, and the sand welcomes it.

What I have done or failed to do has left no noticeable mark on creation. What I do or don't do is of no moment now. Now I am here and grateful to be touched, calmed, and healed by the immense pattern of the universe. And when I die, it will be an honor for my blood to return to the sea and my bones to become the sand. Reassured, I am called back to my life, to another day.

ELIZABETH TARBOX

LIFELINE

Beginnings and endings always seem to capture our imagination and attention. Beginnings and endings hold some secrets that we are forever wanting to reveal. Beginnings and endings give a degree of definition to our lives, and when we encounter reminders of these bookends of life, we can't help but remember something of our own beginnings and wonder about our own endings.

Beginnings and endings have a magic and a mystery that cause us to stop and listen. When we

are in the presence of such moments of transformation, when we publicly and collectively welcome a
baby to the world or grieve a death, when we pri-
vately mark the parting with a friend or the re-birth
of someone's spirit, we feel ourselves drawn into a
profound and compelling encounter with the most
vital and real dimensions of life.

Whenever we witness something of a birth or a
death, a part of us knows we too share in that
moment. In it a part of us may die a little. In it a part
of us could be born again.

Once upon a time someone held us when we
were born. And someday, someone somewhere will
mourn us and miss us. And in between those times,
we move through the seasons of life, and step back
and forth through memory and imagination, from
what was our beginning to what will be our end.

DAVID S. BLANCHARD

INTO THE WILDERNESS

When Jesus was baptized the spirit descended upon
him like a dove and God said, "This is my son, in
whom I am well pleased." It must have been a great
feeling, but it didn't last long. The next thing Jesus
knew, the nice spirit that had descended like a dove

became aggressive and *drove* him into the wilderness. There he spent forty days of deprivation, self-examination, and confrontation with the devil. This was no Sierra Club hike through the Qumran National Forest. He suffered; he struggled; he was tested. Jesus' solitary struggles to remain true to his covenant and calling echo those of his ancestors, who spent forty years in the wilderness establishing a religious community.

Wilderness is a part of every person's soul-journey, and part of our journey together as human beings who seek to live in community. Time in the wilderness is always a time of struggle. It is also a time of transformation and renewal. In traditional terms, it is a time of purification. The journey into wilderness reminds us that we are alone and not alone. We are neither where we have been nor where we are going. There is danger and possibility, risk and promise. In the wilderness, the spirit may descend like a dove and lift us on its wings of hope, then drive us into the depths of despair; it may affirm us with a gift of grace, then challenge us to change. In the stories and rituals of Eastern as well as Western religions, a journey into the wilderness represents a time when we both pursue and resist the Holy.

We may choose to enter the wilderness like the people of Yahweh, to escape bondage, or, like Henry David Thoreau, to "live deliberately." Or we may, like Jesus, be driven there without much choice.

Once there, even our markers of time and space
collapse, for this wilderness is not in space or time,
but is the boundless territory of the soul.

SARAH YORK

FOOTPRINTS

I stare out between the cold points of my coat collar,
never noticing the periphery, intent only on negoti-
ating the uncertainty of the snow-blown path.

Even the frozen earth seems to be on guard, tense
against the slight of another thrust from the rapier
air. Our houses creak and grumble, our cars itch
with winter-thrown dirt, and even our own carefully
nourished bodies feel as if the bones will fragment
like icicles loosed from the roof.

But in my path lie the delicate footfalls of some
creature who owns my yard, owns it every bit as
much as I, but whose presence is betrayed only by
the revealing snow. Who are you, little winter-coated
traveler with the bare toes, too light to break
through the layers of snowflakes, tracking this way
and that in the moonlight, never daring to see if
your fear of me is justified? These fragile prints
sketched on the art-paper brilliance of the snow
remind me that this parcel of land I call my own is

really shared, leased temporarily from the rightful ownership of the natural world.

Slow me down, Spirit of Life, unfreeze my senses: Let me risk a little body heat to look from right to left to see the landscape in all its ice-laced loveliness and to touch my finger to the secret footprint of the nighttime traveler who shares mysterious creation with me.

ELIZABETH TARBOX

THE ART OF FORGIVENESS

Forgiving is a somewhat reckless, typically illogical act. A leap of faith, if you will. When Jesus preached forgiveness, people thought he was insane. Loving your neighbor is one thing, but your enemies too? When struck on one cheek, offer the other? If someone takes your coat, give your cloak as well? We may think it was easy for Jesus to say this, his father being God and all. But what about those of us who live in the real world? Do we have to do it too?

I suppose it depends on what we want from life. Forgiveness in the world is still a bit reckless and illogical. But so is love, having children, or creating anything that we are willing to give away. But we do these things all the time, and we trust that because we have done them, we will be more fulfilled, more connected, more present to the joys and wonders of the world. The alternative is to be satisfied with dismal little corroded existences. But most of the time, we rarely make a conscious choice between the two.

It is through forgiveness that we can discover the freedom it takes to place ourselves in right relation to the divine, with those we love and care about, and with ourselves. It may not be logical, but forgiveness—clear and unconditional—frees the forgiver more deeply than the person being forgiven. Chances are good they didn't even know they had done something that required forgiving. It's a bold and constructive step based in a sense of faith that forgiveness withheld is a poison to the soul. When we hold back forgiveness, we repeat over and over our hurt, reassuring ourselves of our indignation. Some people live their lives off that pain. It's not required. Real power and authentic freedom come with what is so hard to do: forgive.

In the end, those who have found a way to forgive know that the most profound work of forgiveness is done not for those who want it, but for the sake of mending our own soul and for the freedom we find when we recklessly squander our forgiveness.

DAVID S. BLANCHARD

THE LAST SHALL BE FIRST

If there is one spiritual teaching common to all traditions, it must be that we have to lose ourselves in order to find ourselves. If we really want inner peace and purpose, we have to give up our need to succeed. In fact, we have to give up just about any need to be in control of our lives. The Taoist Lao Tse puts it this way:

Therefore the Sage puts himself last, and finds
    himself in the foremost place;
Regards his body as accidental,
    And his body is thereby preserved.
Is it not because he does not live for Self
    That his Self achieves perfection?

Paradoxically, when we let go of the need for power or recognition, we receive it, for we are in harmony instead of in contention with the natural creative principle of the universe. We give up our control and plug into a more natural process. As Chuang Tzu's millipede explains when it is asked how it moves all its legs: "Now all I do is put in motion the heavenly mechanism in me—I'm not aware of how the thing works."

The Taoist sage practices the virtue of "not contending":

The sage acts, but does not possess,
Accomplishes, but lays claim to no credit
Because [she] has no wish to seem superior.

I remember someone who drowned in a river as a hydraulic current drew him under. He drowned because he resisted. If he had moved with the flow of the water, it would have brought him back to the surface.

Think about this: A baby howls, yet its throat never gets hoarse; it makes fists without getting cramped fingers; it stares without blinking.

Or perhaps it is better not to think of it. For common to the sage and the child is the ability to lose the self in harmony with the Tao . . . without having to get it all figured out.

SARAH YORK

MY TESTIMONY

There are many ways to be born again, hopefully not just once or twice. To keep up with the little deaths that come with the passing of time, we ought to get born again as much as time allows. Don't hang around though for God to tap you on the shoulder. Live in the anticipation that it's about to happen at any second, because that's the way it'll be. You'll be reading a book, or listening to some music, when some part of life will suddenly make more sense. You'll awake from a dream and know something you hadn't known before. You'll be making love, or cooking, or carving a pumpkin with a child, or painting, and you will be aware of participating in the creation of something that exists apart from you, and as a part of you at the same time.

There will be times when we all live as exiles. Gay or straight. Believer or nonbeliever. Young or old. Healthy or ill. Brilliant or average. Rich or poor. But the time comes when we are invited to follow a path of reconciliation with all that has been scattered and separated from us. The exile in us can have a long, long way to travel. Some will not go: isolated by hurt, indifferent from disappointment, alienated by anger.

But I don't believe that any of that is the plan. I believe, as surely as I believe anything, that in this life, everything is possible. That is not to say that we will have everything we want, or need, or deserve, but that our souls, the most essential and real dimension of our being, are not confined by the restrictions of the past or the limits of the imagined future. Sometimes that means we live, simply, in hope and trust that the time of renewal, of rebirth, is yet to come. But that it will come if we are alive and aware and receptive.

We have been created to be free.
We have been created to know joy.

We have been created to love.
We were not made to be exiles.

DAVID S. BLANCHARD

MOMENT OF SPIRIT

I have this living image in my mind of the moonlight over the water—a broad highway of the most delicate iridescent light fluidly inviting my participation. It calls and I almost follow; nothing matters but the pull of the moon, and my spirit stretches out for it. Mana, let my spirit soar; for once let my soul go free so I may kiss the moon and become the clouds and roll over the ocean.

But the earth clings to my feet with an insistence that cannot be denied. All I can do is sigh and lean into the music of the moon, and imagine my spirit ghostly and gossamer sliding into the silver night. Then I notice on the edge of the cliff in front of me a single tall blade of grass, leaning likewise and dancing to the same call. We are the earthbound ones, left to keep our adventurous spirits longing and leaning, looking for the light. Keep us poised thus, dear spirit, entrusted to the earth and moving to the poetry of the stars.

ELIZABETH TARBOX

CROWS

I think if I were not a person, I should like to be a bird, and of them all, I should like to be a crow. Crows are big, strutting, powerful birds, gleaming in the right light and not ashamed of the work they do. But I like them most for the way they circle the tall trees and for the way they cry.

I appreciate most those creatures who know how to cry well, and crows do. Catch them at dawn in their ritual grieving, flying over the tall trees, and you'll hear all the sorrow of your heart wrung out and laid before you.

Crows. All my days there have been crows. As a child I awoke to the crying of crows over the neighbor's oak tree, and when I came to America the crows were already here. Buffleheads and egrets are the delight of my bike rides to the beach, but they are still strangers to me, and we are shy and nervous with each other. But the archetypal crow is the cousin of my soul; I long to fly above the maple trees and cry like a crow.

ELIZABETH TARBOX

REVENGE

One October day, just before dinner, in a bit of a
rush, my son Toby, then aged five, and I went up to
the attic to find Halloween costumes. My husband
shouted up that he and Adam would make a run to
the grocery store and do a quick cart's-worth of
shopping. Toby and I unpacked the clown, witch,
and superhero suits, anxious to establish our new
identities before it got any colder or darker, there
being no heat or lights in our attic. Chuck ran to get
his wallet, momentarily folding up the attic stairs as
he went by.

Well, it should have been momentarily. It was
perfectly quiet downstairs. Soon, it was perfectly
dark in the attic. There was no way to get the ladder
unfolded from above. The phone rang. The paper-
boy came to collect. The dog needed to go out. The
water for the broccoli had boiled away. I had a whole
hour to think of an appropriate reaction to my
husband when he walked in the door.

Revenge crossed my mind. I could somehow lure
him into the attic and close it up and see how he
liked it. Good old-fashioned ancient-Greek-type
blood revenge. Or perhaps a little ancient Hebrew
eye-for-an-eye proportional retribution, along the
lines of domestic sabotage—a raw egg in the picnic
lunch, salt in the sugar bowl, that kind of thing.

Then there was forgiveness, Jesus' option. I could just say, "No problem, Chuck, I've never had the opportunity to spend some quiet, dark moments with Toby in our attic before."

Sometimes it's best just to forget. No energy spent on vengeance, no energy spent on forgiving either—a laugh maybe later, nothing more, and it all slips away.

JANE RANNEY RZEPKA

UNTRIED WINGS

UNTRIED WINGS

Hollow bones, streamlined feathers, and wings shaped to push aside the viscosity of air are not what make birds fly.

Birds let go of their grasp on safe perches at the tops of trees because something calls to them. They unfold their untried wings and feel an unimagined power. They soar out, up, and through the winter sky because an ancient longing pulls them home.

Loosed from the sticky grasp of earth, free from the snarls of lesser creatures with daggers in their teeth and muscles in their legs, birds laugh upward, homeward, drawn by a calling which bids them welcome in the sky.

Bird, take me with you when you go. Oh not my lumbering body and knitted tissue, no. Take some other me with you, some invisible soul of me that hears the call you hear, that moves effortlessly with you through the bright pink silk of dawn and the warm butter spread of morning. Carry my longing to be weightless, to move as light moves, to be unseen, scattered through time and space. Teach me to trust my wings.

ELIZABETH TARBOX

IT TAKES ALL KINDS

If it had been left up to me, which I am glad it was not, I probably would have stayed in Europe when my multitude of ancestors were leaving France, England, Wales, and Germany. I would have waved goodbye from the dock and asked them to write. When it comes to drawing the line between the settlers and the pioneers of this world, I usually find myself with those who stay home, bidding farewell from the edge of town at the end of the pier to the more adventuresome pioneers. Neither characteristic is better or worse than the other, but I suspect that each of us would know where we belong. We need both types, even while we feel resentful or jealous of the other's way of life. The damn pioneers drag us off in unknown directions, and the damn settlers dig in their heels and won't budge. But is that all they do?

Where would we be in this world without the pioneers? (I would be a coal-miner in Wales.) Where would we be without people who explore new territories of the world or the mind? (I might be writing with a quill pen.) Where would we be without people who give life its stability, or risk the uncertainty of change? What would life be like without the security fostered by the settlers or the innovations dreamed up by the pioneers? We may

drive each other crazy, but I'm coming to understand that I need the pioneers as much as they need
me to keep life in balance, and to keep the home
fires burning.

DAVID S. BLANCHARD

GOD'S WORK

What is God's work? If God is immanent and tran-
scendent, in and out of everything, then how could
it be possible not to do God's work? Surely all work
is God's work—there is nothing which is not of God.
Is there?

But that doesn't do it, somehow. There are times
when what I do is strictly for me. God or no God,
I'm working for myself, even during those times
when God would probably approve. Mostly what I do
for myself is compatible with what I believe I would
do for God.

But not always. There are times of conflict, when
the prompting and urging of my desire are up
against the sentinel of my conscience. They square
off, these two strong voices somewhere deep in the
thick of me where there is no judge, no referee,
and mercifully no spectators. "Do it," say I. "Don't,"
says God. One of them wins and the other goes

grumbling away, threatening and complaining in the basement of my being like a boiler with an excess of steam. And I am left to live with my decision, to forgive or applaud, to bask in my nobility or blush in my shame. And God and I make peace once more.

Then there are times when I can't tell which is God's voice and which is my own. What about those times when God seems to be saying "Do it" and I am saying "No." When God says, "This is the right thing to do," and I, shaking with fear, confess, "I can't, I'm just too scared."

"I'll be with you."

"How do I know?"

"You can do it, be not afraid."

"I might fail, make a fool of myself."

"Yes, you might. Do it anyway."

"But people might not like me."

"That's right."

"But how do I know this is good? How can I be sure?"

"You cannot be sure. This is a risk."

Yes, those are the toughest times: wanting to do right without losing my safety, not knowing if I am doing God's work, or using God to do mine. There is no superhighway named Right Way. There are no signposts, no guides, no promises, no guarantees; only the lonely voice of conscience and the cringing cry of fear wrestling each other in inner space.

Those are the times of lying awake at night and staring at the detail of the day through a haze of worry, working and reworking the "oughts," the "shoulds," and the "yes, buts" of the thing.

And what's to be done, but to listen to the voice that seems to be speaking a consistent truth, move through the fear to trust the moral judgments we have lived by, and pray for courage.

ELIZABETH TARBOX

ON BEING SCARED

I spent some time this weekend with an old friend, a dentist. She's considering buying her own practice, but wonders if she could retain the current patients and attract new ones. She wonders if the office staff would like her, or befriend her too much, or resent her, or desert her; she wonders about bill collecting, spending too much time on crowns and root canals (which she likes) at the expense of oral surgery (which she doesn't); she wonders about being a good wife and mother and all-around person. She's scared.

My friend is intelligent, well organized, energetic, terrific with teeth . . . but scared. It makes me think we all are. Scared we'll lose the company's big Formica account, scared we'll miss the time change, scared

we're handling the kids' curfew wrong, scared our
money will be in all the dumbest places when tax
laws change, scared of our failing health, scared of
everything falling apart, scared that nobody really
loves us, scared of the fragility of all creation. Scared.

O Spirit of Life and Love, we aren't the giants
we'd like so much to be, and the world can loom so
large. When all is quiet and we are small and the
night is dark, may we hear the tender breathing of
all who lie awake with us in fear, that together we
may gather strength to live with love, and kindness,
and confidence.

JANE RANNEY RZEPKA

STORM WATCH

I was hurting so I went to the beach—the icy beach
with sand pitted by near-frozen spray from an ocean
that roared and rolled and drove a million pebbles
before it.

I hardly noticed the Turner sky and the lonely
beauty of the Gurnet, for the tears on my cheeks
were part wind-wrought and part anger at the
unfairness of a world where good people suffer,
children are hungry, and no one counts the tears.
"Tell me what to do!" I cried, but my voice was thin,

and the words froze in the wind and fell lifeless to the sand.

Then I saw the gulls, two or three, here and there, with that gray-flecked look of fledglings, and I wondered how they survived the brutality of a winter no one warned them would be coming. But gulls ride the waves and face into the wind. They ride each wave as it comes—that is how they do it. It is the only way.

If we follow their example, we will ride the waves, take each new challenge, and face it so we can see what is coming and prepare ourselves. If we stay together and face the wind, we may be able to ride out this storm and the next, until the wind stops roaring and the waves become calm. For all its noise and threat, the ocean encroaches only a few yards up the beach each day before it retreats. If we ride the waves and face the wind, we shall still be together tomorrow when the storm is over and the ocean is quiet.

ELIZABETH TARBOX

HIGH TIDE, LOW TIDE

The bay at high tide is an invitation. It calls and I
follow, falling into the chill wet blanket of motion
and mystery. "Put down your face and stretch out," it
sighs. "Relax, the element is friendly. Swim out to
the raft and fill up your ears; hear the throb of the
ocean massaging the land. Experience the momen-
tary panic of salt water in your nose and mouth; go
on, it's here for you." The bay at high tide is a
sparkle of fiberglass and a slapping of halyards; it's a
rolling, relentless sucking at the shore and uneasy
toeholds on the backs of unseen sea creatures.

But at low tide the sand is strewn with the waves'
forgotten favors. I stand, abandoned like one of the
empty shells, staring out beyond the horizon where
the water receded, where I cannot follow. Low tide is
for reflection and acceptance. I do not belong to
this water world after all. I long to wriggle into the
muddy sand and shoot out tiny fountains like the
clams, but I cannot. I can only stare into the pools
from the salt-spray-softened surface of the beached
raft and let memories bathe me.

There is a time for high tide—being involved and
active, taking risks, and putting out effort to master the
elements—and there is a time for low tide—inactivity
and quiet reflection—and both are necessary in our
lives. May this be a low-tide time for you, when you can

hear the voice of your own calming and thoughtful inspiration, a time when thoughts come uncalled for to comfort or challenge you; and may you go from here renewed and ready to answer the call of your destiny, to jump back into the tide of life once more.

ELIZABETH TARBOX

PARADOX

We named the kitten Puppy Cat, which fits her contradictory nature. She follows us around like a puppy. With no apparent physical needs, she cries for attention. She just wants to chat, and demands some sign that we are listening. If we try to pick her up, however, she protests. "Keep close and pet me," she says, "but don't hold me, I want to be free."

The needs for love and freedom create ambivalence in most of us. Like Puppy Cat, we send out double messages:

Love me . . . but do not intrude upon my space.
I want to be close . . . but I am afraid of being hurt.
I need you . . . but I want to be independent.
I need to be needed . . . but I don't want to be used.

And so on. We live on the boundary of so many inner contradictions. We love the peacefulness of the country . . . and the excitement of the city. We love the freshness of a summer breeze . . . and the beauty of a winter storm.

You can create your own list. We are full of opposing feelings and ideas. The trick is to be able to accept our contradictions and keep them in balance, moving back and forth between them rather than allowing them to lock us in the uncertainty of ambivalence.

There's a difference between ambivalence and paradox. In ambivalence, we are torn—our feelings conflict. In paradox, we accept and admit our own tensions—our feelings generate creative energy from the dynamic of opposites. In ambivalence, we have difficulty making commitments and decisions; we convey double messages to others. In paradox, we admit our uncertainties and reservations and we act, wholeheartedly committing ourselves to our experiences.

Maybe the main difference is that in paradox we are willing to make commitments when all we can ever hope for is partial knowledge and uncertain outcome.

SARAH YORK

SACRIFICE

The old tree standing in our yard saved someone's life today. We were preparing for the forecasted snowstorm, building a fire, planning a cozy day, and watching the first wild flakes when we heard an unmistakable sound. It was the sound of automobile-become-deathtrap, the sound of metal collapsing, cowardly, on impact. We called the police, fetched blankets, and hurried across the lot toward a folded car. Its nose was down, half buried amongst fallen branches and winter-exposed debris.

A man whose truck narrowly missed being in the car crash was already there, pulling open the passenger door. "Are you all right?" he asked to the young woman inside. He eased our blankets over her, and she shivered and nodded and didn't open her eyes. Quickly it seemed there were too many people standing around, needing to be where something bad had happened, needing to be there and not knowing why.

The police and ambulance came and took her away. A wrecker towed the car, and at last the people dispersed. Did the driver of the truck want to come in the house? Was he all right? Yes, he was all right. He said "I'll go home, my wife is waiting for me."

The tree is in pieces. It gave its life. Had it not fractured and fallen when hit by the car, the girl might have died. In sacrifice it looks noble, as if it were part of something dramatic, like the saving of a life.

I don't know if I'm writing about a tree, a car crash, or about being scared. I think we were all scared out there. We said to each other: "She was lucky." But she was not. Had she been lucky, she would not have skidded off the road. She would not have known that sickening, paralyzing moment between out of control and impact. No, she's not all right. I hope tonight she has someone with her who understands that.

ELIZABETH TARBOX

GOD'S LOVE

I'm well loved. That's usually a blessing and a comfort to me. Parents and daughters, lovers and friends, parishioners and colleagues, have shown me many signs of love in all its many guises: gratitude, passion, trust, and comfort. I'm lucky that way, and a more secure man might leave well enough alone. There's just one problem. I've worked long and hard through my life to earn that love. So I've wondered at times where would I be without it?

I really wondered about it when I was coming out. What would become of this carefully constructed world built upon such a deception? Who would love me when I found it so hard to love myself? I learned that God would love me.

Up until then, I had no clue what it meant to experience God's love. If someone told me "God loves you," I would smile outside and feel dismissed inside. And then one day, it was there. God's love. I knew that I was going to be okay. And it didn't depend on my congregation, my family, or my friends. It wasn't a love I had to earn or deserve. It was simply mine, and I felt filled with a kind of peace that the world could neither give nor take away. I call that God's love.

I believe it's there for all of us. Sometimes it needs a place of brokenness to get through. God's love needs the kind of space we create, in spite of our fears, when we are willing to allow what is most authentic about ourselves to be known. When the essence of the one meets the essence of all, it's love at first sight. God loves us for all the right reasons. As for what those reasons are, God only knows.

DAVID S. BLANCHARD

THE GIFT

THE GIFT

Sometimes I think I can teach my children things that will make life better for them as they grow up. I want to believe I can protect them, or that there is some way for me to do their learning for them. This line of thinking is routinely flawed, not because my children are poor learners, but because I'm not always the best teacher. Despite my efforts to avoid repeating mistakes, I'm still learning things I thought I knew. Just last year I mistook a gift for a present.

This gift was a homemade potholder woven of colorful scraps of cloth. It wasn't perfect. It wasn't beautiful. It wasn't particularly unusual. Accepting it as a present, I placed it into service beside the stove.

Four days before Christmas I was called to officiate at a memorial service for a friend. Talking with her five- and nine-year-old daughters, I asked what things they liked to remember about their mom. What things did they do together? What had she taught them? They were busy, deep at work on a gift-making project, but they expressed some memories that mattered, and recounted some gifts their mother had shared with them: making cookies . . . snuggling in bed . . . being their Brownie leader . . . planting bulbs. Then the nine year old looked down and said, "And she taught us how to make these potholders!"

Of course! A gift! How could I miss it?

Presents are the sort of things that fit on lists, complete with size and color preference. Presents are the sorts of things we are smart enough to ask for. Gifts are altogether different. We don't usually think to ask for them, perhaps because we think we don't deserve them, or don't want to risk expressing the need. Maybe we don't even recognize the need ourselves. Gifts differ from presents because no matter what form they take, they always represent something greater, something deeper, something more enduring; they are about things like love, respect, and affirmation.

Gifts given are often woven into some simple token. And sometimes, protecting our own comfort, we give them in disguise. They can be easy to miss.

Now I try to give more gifts than presents, and without too much camouflage. Be gift-bearers yourselves. Give them along with presents, and look carefully for the gifts others are trying to give you.

DAVID S. BLANCHARD

POOR BEAR

A new record was set the other day. An old teddy bear was sold at auction for $65,000. It was made in the 1930s and a gentleman wished to give it to his wife for her birthday, the teddy bear and the wife being the same age. The pre-auction estimate was $1,000.

A romantic might respond "how sweet of that man to spend the equivalent of the gross national product of Burundi on a gift for his wife." A cynic might think less of the expenditure.

Most teddy bears accrue their value to their owners in direct proportion to the amount they are cuddled and hugged, slept with, cried upon, dragged about, and otherwise treasured. The teddy bear in the auction sold for $65,000 because it had never been touched. For over fifty years it sat in a box.

Now, I'm sure that poor teddy bear will get a lot of attention. It'll probably live in a display case and have its own insurance policy. But it'll never know the purposes for which it was created. It'll never be loved. For all those years, overlooked and forgotten. And forevermore, too valuable to be loved.

One could disparage the values of a society in which such extravagance exists. One could conclude that the owners confirm the wisdom that a fool and his money are soon parted. But the more I think about it, all I can think is, poor bear.

DAVID S. BLANCHARD

LOOKING FOR LOVE IN ALL THE WRONG PLACES

Most of us look for love in only the most obvious places, and as a result, most of us come away disappointed. It's as if we are still grade school kids, counting valentines as a measure of what matters. The love that matters is not typically the subject of sonnets or love songs.

There can be love in being told we are wrong. There can be love in sharing a regret. There can be love in asking for help. There can be love in communicating hurt. There can be love in telling hard truths. Most of us find it painful to live at this level of love, but it can be there, even in these most unlikely places. It isn't the kind of love we've been promised in the fairy tales of princes and fairy godmothers, but it is the kind experienced by frogs and dwarfs. It's the sort of love that can bring us closer to finding the missing pieces of ourselves that we need to make us whole.

Some of the most loving things I've ever experienced, I haven't been ready for, wasn't looking for, and nearly didn't recognize. A few of them I didn't want. But all of them have changed me, transformed some part of me, filled in a place that I didn't even know was empty.

When the valentine has been tucked away in a drawer, the candy eaten, the flowers faded and gone,

there will be other legacies of love that will last as
long as we do, because they have brought us to know
an element of life—part feeling, part idea, part
mystery—that once known, is ours to keep.

DAVID S. BLANCHARD

TWO BOXES OF NOSTALGIA

Two boxes of Girl Scout cookies arrived.

"Why did you buy *two* boxes?" my husband asked.

"Because there were *two* children selling them," I
replied.

When I bite into one of those delicious cookies, I
remember the time in fifth grade that I peddled
cookies with my best friend. In those days, we just
took the boxes out and sold them—no orders. We
stopped off to rest, and devoured an entire box of
cookies. I understand why they take orders now.

I remember some of the things I learned as a Girl
Scout—how to make my own stove out of cardboard
and wax and a tuna can. How to tie three sticks
together to hold a bowl of water. And how to choose
a site for a latrine . . . and how to make the latrine.

Then there were the badges. One I earned for
learning how to grow something from seed. With my
mother's help, I chose nasturtiums. I remember the

day I planted them, the day I saw the first sprouts, the day buds appeared . . . and the day that I noticed that they had withered from neglect.

I also earned the cooking badge. "Keep the fire low and turn the bacon frequently," my mother said. I tried that for a few minutes, then lost patience and turned the fire up. When I received the badge, there were still scars where the grease had attacked my arm. Withered flowers, burned bacon, and all . . . I still got the badges. That's because what we learn in the process is always more important than the way things come out.

SARAH YORK

A DRIVER'S LICENSE AND A MAJOR CREDIT CARD

For years I kept a check for $250 that was returned to me for nonpayment of funds. Account closed. Address unknown. I had not written down the number of a driver's license. I kept the check to remind me of how foolish I had been to trust a stranger.

On a recent visit to the library, I approached the librarian with an armful of books on Native American religion. As she stamped them, I reached for my card. "You won't need that today," she said. "Our computer is down." I wondered if she would ask me to write down my name and the titles of the books, but she didn't. I had an awkward feeling as I walked through the door with all those books; I might get fined if I brought them back late, but there would be no consequences if I did not bring them back at all. All day long, books were leaving the library and borrowers were trusted to return them.

That evening I went to pick up the carpet I had selected for my new office. I did not yet have a check from the church to pay for it, and explained to the salesperson that I did not have the money. Did he want me to pay for it myself, or should I pick it up in a few days? No, he said. Just take the carpet and send the check.

Twice in one day I was not asked for a driver's license and a major credit card. Not until I experienced all this trust in a single day did I think about how the attitude of distrust prevails in our everyday dealings with strangers.

Trust is hard to build. When it is broken, it is even more difficult to rebuild. Yet we know from our intimate relationships as well as our casual transactions with strangers that trust is essential to any community. No wonder we have so much trouble making treaties with foreign nations when we cannot even trust our own neighbors.

I have thrown away that check for $250. I may get taken again, but I would rather keep the memory of a day at the library and the carpet store to remind me of the hope that exists for community.

SARAH YORK

WHAT ARE YOU SAVING IT FOR?

I was trying to write when my niece, who was getting ready to go back to college, interrupted me.

"Can I have this?" she said, holding up a rug that had been handed down in the family. "No," I said, "That is a genuine Navajo rug—it's very valuable. You don't put a rug like that on the floor."

"How about this?" she asked, displaying a large piece of material my husband had brought back for me from a trip to India. "It would look great on the couch."

"I really don't want that to be worn out," I said.

"Well, what about this?"

"You don't walk on a rug like that. . . ."

"And these?"

"You don't put old quilts like those on beds. . . ."

Finally she gave up. "Why do you just keep all these things stored away in a closet where no one can enjoy them?" she asked. "What are you saving them for?"

It was a good question. I thought of the unpolished silver and the glass objects safely shut away. I remembered my own sermon on gifts—about how the best gifts we receive are the ones we cannot keep. I made my point by burning a lovely candle that had been given to me. I watched it melt and I told the story of how the cat broke a little clay dog my father had given me, and how I cried. Then I talked about what was really important about the gift. It was a gift of memory—of my Great Dane, who liked to sit in people's laps, and slobbered all over the furniture. It was a gift of talent—the skills of an artist who could bring life to an image. It was a gift of time—time taken to shape something special from a lump of clay; time taken to wrap it carefully and mail it. And it was a gift of self. Memory, talent, time, self . . . none of these, I said in the sermon, broke when the cat sent the clay image crashing to the floor. It is dangerous, I said, to allow things to embody the sentiment that is precious to us.

"What are you saving it for?" The question stirs me. Those old things are valuable . . . but I don't plan to sell them. I am saving them for the sake of saving them—to hold onto something of the past.

My niece still needs an answer. I guess I will have to let her take one of those precious old things. And maybe, if she puts it away where it doesn't get too much use, she will still have it when one of her children asks her the same question.

SARAH YORK

THE PILLOW

Last summer, when our family was visiting Maine, we slept wonderfully well. We just couldn't get over how soft the pillows were! I was so impressed, in fact, that I dug out a Vermont Country Store catalog and immediately ordered a couple of feather pillows—the softest they make.

One fine day the pillows arrived. After a lot of fanfare, I curled up for a nap, and yes, it was indeed the softest, most restful pillow on earth.

But it smelled funny.

The pillow drove me crazy. I couldn't place the smell—but finally, lying there half-awake one night, the smell took me to Wisconsin, to my sister's farm. I knew what the feather pillow smelled like. It smelled like a chicken coop!

Sometimes in life we get exactly what we ask for. I ordered a feather pillow and I got a pillow that smelled like feathers. We get what we thought we wanted; it doesn't seem right somehow; and the problem is so obvious that we can't even see it—or smell it. Whoever said that we make the bed and then have to lie in it, has a point.

JANE RANNEY RZEPKA

WINDOW OR AISLE?

"Window or aisle?" the man at the counter asked as I prepared to board the plane for Detroit.

No matter how often I fly, I always pause to make the choice: To take a window seat means being able to get a God's eye view of earth. But what if I want to go to the restroom? It's such a bother to have to ask people to move. And I don't like feeling trapped.

My answer is always the same: "Window." To choose the window is to choose to see. Whether I am identifying a river or marveling at the play of moonlight on the ocean; whether the view is a patchwork of planted fields, a city showing off its neon finery, or a comforter of clouds, I am filled with a deep sense of awe. Sometimes, as the plane moves through a storm, breaking through the clouds and into the sun, my own spirit opens up to invite in the expanse of beauty. There is always something to see—always something I have never seen before.

Knowing that to choose the window is an invitation to beauty, awe, and wonder—that it is even an opportunity to break through the cloudiness of my own spirit—why do I always pause to make the decision? Each time we get a seat on a plane we are invited to choose to be touched by the world or to remain complacent and take it for granted. We are invited to choose beauty or fear, vision or convenience. Each day of our lives, in fact, we are given the choice, "Window or aisle?" Something inside me will always pause before I choose . . . but I think I'll take the window.

SARAH YORK

MARSUPIAL SHELL

The shell on my desk is long and rolled up. I don't know its name or where it came from, only that it is here, and beautiful biscuit shades wave over it in perfect parallel lines. Within its folds nestle two other tiny round shells. They are safe there, protected.

How we long to stay in the firm grasp of someone else's arms, to be swept up in their adventure and protected like these fragile twins in the shell's embrace, to be cared for, to be encircled, to sleep secure.

But there is another way of seeing the ocean's artwork. Those little shells are stuck. Somehow, sometime, they were washed inside the other's grip and nothing, neither the action of the ocean nor the roughness of the beach upon which the family foundered, can set them free without breaking the shell which protects them. As long as they remain as they are, they will not grow.

Perhaps we are like the shells, wanting as parents to hold on to those for whom we feel responsible;

wanting our babies not to take on the uncertainty of
life alone. But I believe that relationships were not
meant to be as rigid or confining as the sculpture of
these three shells. We are swept up in the open ocean
of adulthood, formed by the elements of work and
play, shaped by the holding on and the letting go,
smoothed and wrinkled by saying hello and saying
good-bye. Each of us deserves a separate, special life,
with love enough to protect but not disfigure us.

Creator Spirit, grant us the strength to know
when to hold on to our dear ones and when to let
them go; provide us the protection of loving arms
which give us the security to choose our freedom;
and when we come to rest at last, let it be in the
calm of some safe harbor.

ELIZABETH TARBOX

NOT FOUND

Something happened the other day that has made
me wonder if maybe machines are not only smarter
than people, but wiser. The machine in question is
my office computer.

There are many things it can do that I cannot, and
probably never will. My computer has a memory that
exceeds anything I could ever hope for. It remembers

things I would rather it (and I) could forget: half-baked sermons, memos about old problems, letters I wished I hadn't sent. It's all there. Billions of bytes of information preserved until I can figure out how to send them to that big deletion in the sky.

Besides having a memory that runs circles around me, it's a mean speller. (I'm not.) Thier? Their? Friend? Freind? I know the rules. I was present in third grade: "I" before "e" except after "c," etc., etc., etc. The fact that *I* knew what *I* meant didn't impress my earliest teachers. My computer doesn't mark off for spelling, and for that I am grateful.

But about the smart computer being wise. I was proofing a document and the spell-checker came back to me with the message "Not found." The word was misery. M-I-S-E-R-Y. Hmm. Does it require an "a" instead of an "e"? No. I had actually spelled it correctly. "Nice work, David," I thought. Outsmarting the computer! Then I began to think about it.

What's the message here? What's this business, "Not found"?

Could it be that misery really does love company, usually ours? Could it be that we sometimes go looking for it to give ourselves some strange sense of companionship? What would happen if we stopped looking? Or started to look for something else? What if our brains came back to us with the message "Not found" the next time we sought the company of misery? Maybe, just maybe, my computer was giving me the message I needed to hear. I think I'll leave misery alone, and hope it won't find me either.

DAVID S. BLANCHARD

NOTES FROM THE ZOO

I spent a day at the Brooklyn Zoo. It just happened that way. And when it happens that a minister spends the day at the zoo, I believe it is customary for that minister to observe that animals remind one so much of people (though not, of course, of members of the congregation).

Well, it's true. We and the other animals have a lot in common, a lot to discuss, and a lot to learn from each other. In the brand new jungle exhibits, I learned three things (which far exceeds my usual learning limit during days off with the family).

An elephant's gestation period is almost two years. Two years, according to the guide, is a pretty long time to be pregnant. (I had to agree.) But eventually, after what must take enormous patience and some very hard work on the big day, a beautiful infant weighing at least 125 pounds is born. The elephants reminded me that big, beautiful projects, of nearly any description, require a long wait.

I saw a rhinoceros up close. It's skin seemed thicker than any skin I'd seen on anything during my thirty-five years. The guide knew people take one look and think "thick skin," so he told us how sensitive rhino skin is to sun and insect bites. The rhinos reminded me that the thick-skinned feel pain like the rest of us.

The tapir looks like a gigantic pig and escapes extinction in several countries where, for religious reasons, people avoid eating pork. But tapirs are actually related not to pigs, but horses. The tapir reminded me that the right thing often happens for the wrong reason.

A foliage tour on Columbus Day? Maybe, but I recommend the zoo.

JANE RANNEY RZEPKA

FILING FOR AN EXTENSION

Death and taxes. As the saying goes, these are the only things in life that we don't have any choice about. We can, however, file for extensions. Postponement gives us a little more time to get our act together.

We opted for postponement when our dog was diagnosed with bone cancer. We had her leg amputated, knowing that she would live perhaps six months more. Then we prepared ourselves for the loss.

We don't always have the option of filing for an extension when it comes to facing death. Some of us will have time to prepare; others will be snatched away without warning. The important thing is to live so that death doesn't make us feel cheated. I remember the lines from *Hamlet*:

There is special providence in the fall of a sparrow.
If it be now, tis not to come;
if it be not to come, it will be now;
if it be not now, yet it will come.
The readiness is all.

The readiness is all. The readiness has more to do with life than death. It has to do with knowing that we have said what we need to say to people we love; it has to do with knowing we are doing more with our days than surviving; it has to do with acting upon our values now and not waiting for the day when we have more time. Yes, it has to do with life.

I am glad April 15 only happens once a year. Still, it isn't so bad to be reminded once a year to live in readiness for the time when we will not have the option of filing for an extension.

SARAH YORK

A SPORT FOR LIFE

In a homework assignment designed to appeal to the sports-minded of the fourth graders, my son Toby's class was asked to make collages: "Use magazine pictures that show the sports activity you think you'd like best when you grow up." The collages poured in the next morning, snipped out dreams of pro football, baseball, and, from those children edging over four feet tall, basketball.

Toby chose pig-racing. Pig-racing!

I like that in a kid. Already, Toby knows that while popular sports are okay, he's apt to find a better dream for himself if he uses a little imagination.

I hope he remembers that lesson in life: to search out just the right dream, one that offers a pace and challenge that suits him, in spite of the choices others may make. Plenty of folks run around dribbling and punting and touching all the bases. But somebody's got to race those pigs. May it be my son.

JANE RANNEY RZEPKA

THE LESSON OF THE DEER

> We shall not cease from exploration,
> And the end of all our exploring
> Will be to arrive where we started
> *And know the place for the first time.*
> —T. S. ELIOT, "LITTLE GIDDING"

I went to the woods because, like Thoreau, I wanted to "live deep and suck out all the marrow of life." On the final morning of my sojourn, four deer tiptoed across the clearing in front of my cabin, then disappeared into the trees. I tiptoed into the woods to catch another glimpse of these lovely animals. Unrewarded, I returned to the house. As I approached, the frightened deer looked up from the clearing for a moment before they darted silently into the trees once again. If only I had stayed!

We learn the lesson of the deer over and over. Off we go in pursuit of our dreams, only to find that what we wanted was in front of us all along. I wonder how many times we search far away for what is at home before we stay and receive it. I wonder how many times we look outside of ourselves for fulfillment before we realize that it is inside. Perhaps this lesson is one we always know, but never really learn.

SARAH YORK

BETWEEN SEASONS

BETWEEN SEASONS

Tiny sparkles from diamond drops of ice high up in the naked branches of the maple and elm reflect the sun through my window and work at distracting me.

Beneath their frozen coats, the tiny buds of spring wait to be born, but winter has one last picture to show me before spring comes laughing to the trees. As if they were working together in this month between seasons—sunshine, catbirds, and crocuses for spring, and icicles hanging on pine needles and cardinals picking sunflower seeds off the snow-drifted bird feeder for winter—the two seasons call forth from me a great Amen.

Here we are then, between seasons, not knowing for sure what to do next. Do we conserve and play it safe against an unexpected onslaught striking us like one last winter blast, or do we cast off our coats and take a risk, daring to embrace a spring which is not quite here? Thank God we have each other and this place of worship to come to, when we need to make decisions in our search for both security and renewal. May we remember in the chilliest winter storm or the balmiest spring morning that this place is here for us, that here we share in creation's love no matter what the season.

ELIZABETH TARBOX

SEASON OF MUD

A friend of mine from Maine says that down east there are five seasons: summer, fall, winter, spring, and mud. Mud is the season between winter and spring, the season of melting snow when winter's icy grip loosens its hold . . . but doesn't quite let go.

When I lived near the bay that divides the eastern end of Long Island into two forks, I witnessed the beginning of this fifth season in a phenomenon which Thoreau describes as the "thundering" of the ice. Dressed for insulation from the February wind, I walked on the snow-covered beach. A sharp cracking sound boomed from beneath the frozen stillness of the bay's surface. I marveled with Thoreau: "Who," he asks, "would have suspected so large and thick-skinned a thing to be so sensitive?" The beach resembled an arctic glacier, large chunks of ice reflecting both sun and sky. They imposed a barrier between sand and sea that appeared invincible even though it was disappearing every moment. Many white ice-rafts drifted with the current while a flock of ducks squawked noisily above.

Two weeks later only a remnant of the imposing glacier remained, and the shoreline was visible again. I could stroll along a thin strip of sand between the water and the ice. I thought of the paradoxes of this in-between season when the rigid is juxtaposed with the fluid; when spring's warmth softens the winter earth and winter's chill snatches back the spring air; when each day is an unpredictable and unreliable combination of what was and what will be.

The season of mud begins with thunder and announces change; it is the season of transition. Transitions are times when the thick skin of habit that protected us surrenders to the possibilities of growth and renewal. The inner thawing renders us sensitive and vulnerable to the unpredictable, until we emerge comfortably into new ways of being. We aren't sure who we are or where we will end up.

In the midst of the mud and muddle of all transitions, the seeds of promise stir quietly beneath the surface like spring bulbs drinking the snow.

SARAH YORK

PASSOVER

L'sho-noh ha-bo-oh bee-ru-sho-lo-yeem.

May Zion be blessed with peace, and may our brethren and all humankind live in harmony and contentment.
Amen.

—BENEDICTION FROM THE PASSOVER HAGGADAH

The Jewish festival of Passover is known as "the Season of Our Freedom." Recalling their ancestors' release from bondage and oppression in Egypt, the people celebrate liberation. As the earth is released from the grip of winter, humanity celebrates release from bondage.

But the story doesn't stop with release. After terrible plagues and the exodus from Egypt, Pharaoh's army chased the people to the Red Sea, where the waters parted for the Hebrews, then flowed back to swallow up the Egyptian soldiers and their chariots.

Entering the wilderness, the people complained ("murmured") to Moses that it was his fault they were in this awful place, hungry and tired and thirsty.

This was only the beginning. The people murmured a lot in the wilderness. They recognized that bondage had been pretty secure. Life in slavery was a drag, but at least they knew what each day would bring, and a few conveniences had made their burdens easier to bear. Freedom sounded great when they were slaves, but now that the people had to set up camp and find food in a strange land, they weren't so sure.

It is safer to stay where things are familiar and events are predictable. It is safer to be in bondage. Freedom means risk; it means pursuing a dream of a promised land that we may never reach. One Jewish legend tells that even after Moses said words to part the sea, the waters did not recede until the first Hebrew placed a foot in the water.

The Passover Seder is a thanksgiving meal—a time to express gratitude to the God who hears the cries from all who are oppressed and exploited. It is a time to express regret for the suffering of all who pay the price for freedom, including those we call the enemy. And it is a time to express commitment to a vision of the promised land. For in the ritual of gratitude and remembering comes courage—the courage to put our feet in the water and take risks again and again for freedom.

SARAH YORK

GOOD FRIDAY

Eli Eli lema sabachthani.
—MATTHEW 27:46

"My God, My God, why hast thou forsaken me?" Jesus cried out these words in his own language, Aramaic. This is one of only a few places in the gospels where Jesus' own language is preserved. Strong words. Memorable words.

Jesus was alone. Judas had betrayed him; the disciples had disappeared; and Peter—the faithful

Peter who would become the foundation of the church—denied knowing him. At this moment of deepest need, God had run out on him too. Jesus was alone.

Some time ago, I sat by the bedside of a woman who was forty-five and dying painfully of cancer. She had a lot more living to do. But each day, more life slipped away, and she wailed. Not cried. Not wept. She *wailed* through the agony—a wail of despair that defies translation. Here was a highly successful woman. She was loved dearly by family and friends. But in her dying, she was alone. And so she prayed; she cried out wordlessly to the absent God.

This is the paradox. In our despair, we are moved to pray, even if our prayer is no more than a cry of rage against the forces of life in which we have placed our trust. In suffering, like Jesus, we feel alone and forsaken. But in suffering we turn to the absent God, and in our inarticulate utterings, declare God to be present.

That does not mean that we feel the presence; it does not insure that there is a presence; it only insists that deep in the empty soul full of absence, a wail is addressed to God and no one but God understands it because no one else knows the language.

SARAH YORK

ROLLING AWAY THE STONE

In the tomb of the soul, we carry secret yearnings, pains, frustrations, loneliness, fears, regrets, worries.

In the tomb of the soul, we take refuge from the world and its heaviness.

In the tomb of the soul, we wrap ourselves in the security of darkness.

Sometimes this is a comfort. Sometimes it is an escape. Sometimes it prepares us for experience. Sometimes it insulates us from life.

Sometimes this tomb-life gives us time to feel the pain of the world and reach out to heal others. Sometimes it numbs us and locks us up with our own concerns.

In this season where light and dark balance the day, we seek balance for ourselves.

Grateful for the darkness that has nourished us, we push away the stone and invite the light to awaken us to the possibilities within us and among us—possibilities for new life in ourselves and in our world.

Amen.

SARAH YORK

HUMANIZING MOM

On Mother's Day, one expects to read about the wonder and glory of motherhood. While I can tell you from personal experience that we mothers like to be appreciated, I can also tell you that a rosy and sentimental Mother's Day column always refers to mothers in some other family—the picture painted there is not me, not my mom, not my grandmothers.

In my family, mothers do not suffer any more than other mortals, nor are we particularly unsung. We complain when we trip over shoes on the living room floor, and we expect a little praise for carrying the daily Grand Accumulation at the bottom of the stairs up the aforementioned stairs.

We do not deserve or expect devotion from our children. We wanted to have children. It was our idea. If they come around from time to time when they are grown-ups, we are ever so glad. But if they live their lives as secure and independent souls, we value that.

Motherhood, in my family, is not always the most important job in the world. Some of us are actually good at it, some of us shuffle along and do our best, and a few are better off in other professions. We try to face that.

Mother's Day is no time to romanticize parenthood—parenting is a down-to-earth process if ever there was one. So this Mother's Day, let's humanize Mom. Thank her for doing what she could, given all the dirty socks, thank her for loving you as well as she was able in spite of your three years in junior high, and then, let her thank you for the privilege of being your mother.

JANE RANNEY RZEPKA

FATHER'S DAY

Creator, whom some call Father, we are gathered here to worship together on a day set aside to recognize and praise all fathers. It is easy, God, to thank our perfect father, the one who was unfailingly wise and kind, who worked hard all day and still had time to play baseball or take us out for ice cream in the evening. We are eager to thank the father who showed us by example what responsible citizenship is, who laughed and cried with us as he read us our bedtime story, who shared his problems with us and trusted us with his feelings, who set us firmly on the road to adulthood and knew just when to hug us close and when to let us go.

But we have a harder time knowing what to say to our imperfect father, the one who struggled and fell short or didn't seem to care at all. There are no cards to tell the father who treated us unkindly that the wound is still open. We are hardly granted permission on Father's Day, or at any other time, to tell our father that we really wanted to love him but he wouldn't let us get that close, or that we really wanted his love but he hurt us instead.

God, today, grant us a measure of peace with our memories and our feelings. If there can be reconciliation with our imperfect father, honesty, forgiveness, and healing, then let it be so; but if that is not possible, then at least let us find peace with ourselves. Let part of our maturity be the acceptance of the reality that father-son and father-daughter relationships can be destructive, and that it is not our fault. If our father was or is a source of discomfort to us, then let us know that that is a truth which may not be changed. We cannot change our father; we can only change ourselves, and then only after we have understood the truth and grieved over our hurts.

So God, today, bless our fathers—all of them. Lead us to a true appreciation of their qualities and a recognition of their frailties. Let us stop expecting more than our fathers can give and start giving what we can to them. And let us remember that we can learn how to parent from all the examples shown to us, the good and the bad.

ELIZABETH TARBOX

BORED SILLY

Did you know that July is National Hot Dog Month? It is. It is also National Eye Exam Month, Minority Tourism Month, Hitchhiking Month, National Baked Bean Month, National Ice Cream Month, National July Belongs to Blueberries Month, National Lamb and Wool Month, National Peach Month, National Picnic Month, National Purposeful Parenting Month, National Recreation and Parks Month, National Tennis Month, Sports and Recreation Books Month, and it is also National Anti-Boredom Month. There seems to be something for everyone. I figure I'll do my part in celebrating about half of these commemorations before the month is out. A picnic with a well-stacked cooler would take care of many, and if you hitchhiked to the park in a wool sweater and brought a book about sports and an optometrist along you'd be well on your way to a thorough celebration of July. The only festival I plan to omit from my July is the last one mentioned: National Anti-Boredom Month. I think July is a wonderful time to be bored.

In spite of what they hold as true at The Boring Institute of Maplewood, New Jersey, summertime is the ideal season for boredom. Some people call it vacation. I think being bored is an undervalued state of mind. Obviously, it's not a place one wants to stay all the time, but only when you're bored do you let yourself fully pay attention. When you're a kid that's when you lie on the ground and watch the industry of ants, or look for shapes in the clouds, or find four leaf clovers, or make up a game with whoever's hanging around. Later on in life, it's when, well, it's when you do the same sort of stuff. But while you're watching the ants or scouring the skies, you're also imagining all kinds of other things, making connections, sorting out your life, sensing the patterns that give your life its shape. That doesn't happen when you're in a hurry. It doesn't happen when every day has a full agenda. Those things rarely happen when you want to make them happen.

Boredom is one of those gifts life gives us that we often think we'd just as soon do without, and it would surely be a curse if it was unrelieved. But for most of us, it's a temporary state of grace that we visit from time to time, temporarily without our bearings, when we discover all the ways we human creatures are made for wonder.

As summer arrives, I anticipate a good boring July. This is our opportunity for authentic boredom. After all, everyone knows August is National Canning Month, so you know we'll be busy then.

DAVID S. BLANCHARD

INVOCATION

The leaves abandon themselves to the metamorphosis of the season, and I want to be like them, to open my arms and float on the supporting wings of expectation to whatever comes next. But I cling to the branch of my old ways, long after I know that it is not where I belong. I watch a chipmunk jumping and foraging, darting about in a fine combination of playfulness and planning, and I want to be like the chipmunk, enjoying my work for what it is. But my need for security keeps me on guard and unable to give myself to the moment for fear of sacrificing the future. I admire the brilliant moon watchful of the night, and I want to be like the moon, serene, present, and dependable. But my fear and my longing keep me restlessly in motion and unable to give or receive the love that the world knows.

Dear God who lives and works in human hearts and acts with human hands, whose touch is on every fallen leaf, give me strength to trust you. Let me remember in my darkest hours that life is renewing itself in each moment and with that renewal comes forgiveness and a fresh chance to try again. I am so resilient to life's lessons at times when I ought to bow before them, and so fragile at those moments when I ought to stand strong. Spirit of Life, I ask this morning that I may draw strength from this place, this sacred space set among the fallen leaves and the playful chipmunks, and beneath the benevolent caress of the moon.

ELIZABETH TARBOX

BURSTS OF SPLENDOR

On an airplane recently I sat next to a science teacher from San Francisco. Twenty-four years old, flying east for the first time, the young man was eager to experience autumn. He'd never seen leaves change color.

He went on and on about this: "In pictures, some of the leaves look red. I just can't believe they could turn bright red!" I, meanwhile, was trying to write a meditation for Sunday morning, along the lines of appreciating the glory and the beauty that is ours at this time of year—I wanted him to pipe down. But no, he continued with his incredulity, his delight, his boyish anticipation of the prospective spectacle.

I couldn't imagine the young science teacher happier than he already was, but as he spoke to me of his plan for his friends, he really began to glow. He had decided that he would choose one special brilliantly colored leaf for each friend, and make a little gift of it when he returned home. In six weeks.

Teacher of science though he was, he hadn't
learned that bursts of splendor never last. He was
too young, I guess, and too giddy.

And I couldn't tell him.

Spirit of transient joy,
Spirit of utter delight,
Our hearts are often anguished and bruised.
May we embrace your glorious moments as if they
     were forever,
And if we be too innocent, may we be gently forgiven.

JANE RANNEY RZEPKA

RETURN TO CHAOS

I looked out the window, surprised to see winter's
first snowfall. I wasn't ready.

"Have you seen my boots anywhere?" I asked my
husband Chuck, after I had searched for them in
every logical location in the house.

Forty-five minutes of climbing over boxes in the
attic ("Here's the Christmas wrapping we couldn't
find last week"), rummaging through closets ("I've
looked there twice already, but you can go ahead
and look anyway"), and sneezing into the dust under
beds ("Where did all *this* come from?") yielded only
frustration. No boots.

It was Chuck who finally found the boots. I had given up after six trips to the attic, two trips to the basement, and multiple closet checks. The terrible truth is that they were in the attic in a box labeled "Camping Equipment," well hidden underneath a tent and a Coleman stove.

The fact is, we humans do not like to live in the kind of disorder where winter boots can get lost in a box of camping equipment. We are particularly uncomfortable when such disorder originates in our own minds.

But there it is, the terrible truth—or half of it, anyway. The other half is that once such a lapse of logic has taken place, a *return* to disorder is the only avenue of correction. It was only because Chuck could imagine the most illogical location for the boots that he could discover them.

Logic is useful, most of the time. But sometimes a return to chaos has its logic, too.

SARAH YORK

MYTH AND MIRACLE

This is going to sound like an Easter message, a trifle defensive in tone, that responds to the imaginary critics who chastise us for finding meaning in the Easter story though we may not believe it happened. Or they tease us about our icky spring/bunny/daffodil talk, as though we're trying to celebrate Easter, but doing it wrong. About the time my spirit wants to soar with Alleluias and rebirth, with myth and natural miracle, those imaginary voices complain about Biblical literalism on the one hand or plain theological denial on the other.

Christmas works the same way. Myth and nature. We have a religious story of the birth of a holy baby, and we have the miracle of the lengthening days. Critics like to smirk at one or the other. But not me. I go for the myth and the miracle one hundred percent.

A baby was born, the story goes. The baby was special. The baby would bring peace and justice and love. Everyone around was amazed by the child, awed. The baby brought hope. The people knew joy. I love this story. I love it not because I believe a virgin bore a Newborn King on 12/25/0; I love it because it reminds me of the ancient wisdom of celebrating human greatness and holiness.

And the lengthening days. The lengthening days! How can anybody say "Bah humbug" to the very light itself? Together on Christmas we light our little candles so that the world might seem less bleak, we might feel less afraid, and flickers of safe expectation might again come our way.

I can't think why I'd want to hold back at
Christmastime. So I wish you each a season full of
infant-hope and steady light. Merry Christmas!

JANE RANNEY RZEPKA

THE CHRISTMAS SPIRIT

Newsletters from other churches arrive in the mail
every day. So I read them, and they get me to
thinking. For example:

Ministers' columns at this time of the year say one
of two things: "The holiday season is a happy time,"
or "The holidays are depressing." The "happy time"
school of thought makes a case for generosity, good
cheer, and a deepening spirituality, whereas the
"depression" advocates cite studies that prove the
winter holidays are difficult. At the moment, the
"happy holidays" group has a slight edge, the fresh-
est crop of Ph.D.s having studied our December
moods and found them to be merry after all.

I beg to differ. With no empirical work at all to
back me up, I'd like to make a case for people being
regular people even when December rolls around.
Sure, Mom is frantic after Thanksgiving, but she is a
frantic person in general. Brother John is noncha-
lant about the holidays, but he's always been the

laid-back type. Aunt Martha gears up for a family squabble, but remember, she set up a round or two in July. Uncle John is a natural Santa, but he's a sweetie all year long.

In our family, we will incessantly exclaim, "Where's your Christmas spirit?" from Thanksgiving until the twenty-fifth. This phrase, at our house, has always been an obnoxious code for "Lighten up, it's Christmastime, act merry, not human."

I'm changing the code. This year "Christmas spirit" will refer to the fact that we are who we are, merry or depressed, and we love each other anyway.

JANE RANNEY RZEPKA

GREAT GIFTS UNDER $25

The perennial question is how to avoid being overwhelmed by the holiday season. Far be it from me to suggest that this is a "woman's question," but a glance at the newsstand reveals these feature articles in December's women's magazines: "300 Ideas for the Best and Happiest Christmas Ever" (*Family Circle*); "323 Great Gifts for Under $25" (*Good Housekeeping*); "112 Cookie Recipes" and "10 Ways to Look Dazzling for the Holidays" (*Ladies' Home Journal*); and "50 Ways to Cut Holiday Costs"

(*Woman's Day*). Does this look like holiday spirit to you? To me it looks like work—if not guilt, anxiety, and confusion.

I don't mean to be a Scrooge; I love the winter holidays. My goals, however, are less ambitious than the magazines': I'd be happy with only one or two ideas for a "very good" Christmas; one real possibility for a gift under $25; one good cookie recipe that doesn't call for refrigerating the dough; and a few ways to look alert and alive ("dazzling" is out of the question) for the holidays.

The *Boston Globe*'s "Confidential Chat" column suggests we save this year's wrapping paper to glue on next year's Kleenex boxes. No one suggests paying some attention to the haunting vision that appeared to the Judean shepherds almost 2,000 years ago, or to the universal significance of the ancient December festivals of darkness and light. Few articles remind us of the simple beauty of a wreath or the memories that the old songs and stories unearth. Good will and giving are overlooked. These, to me, are the "ideas for the best and happiest holiday season ever." These are the "great gifts under $25."

JANE RANNEY RZEPKA

UNEXPECTED NEW YEAR

I write this, and you will read it, at the start of a "new" year. I say "new," because that is how it has been parceled out in the proper number of days and weeks and months to make a year. One is over. One is beginning. For the next couple of weeks we will all persist in writing the wrong year on checks and letters. Quickly, the new year will become simply this year, and the old year will become attached to all that's past.

To me, New Year's Eve has always seemed a rather arbitrary festival. A grand excuse for a good party. A useful time for reflection. An occasion for resolutions to be made, or at least toyed with, for the future. I don't subscribe to the notion of time that the new year traditionally promotes, with the old geezer being shown the door as the young tyke in diapers makes her entrance. I think that time accumulates for each of us, and that the slate is never made blank. It's more like a mural that we keep adding panels to, bending around the corners of our lives.

There are such things as "new years" in all of our lives. But rarely do I think they begin and end according to the Roman calendar. They begin and end, at times by choice and at times by chance, at rather arbitrary moments of transformation. Perhaps in a moment of loss. Other times when we feel in control of our lives and make a decision to live differently. Maybe in that rare moment when we know we are in love. Or when we begin a new job, have a baby, write a poem, change our mind, get sick, lose a friend, look in a mirror. You'll know the time. You'll know when your own "new year" has begun. When it happens, raise a toast, throw confetti, wear a funny hat, blow on a noisemaker. It'll be time to mark. Even if it's July. Especially if it's July. Happy New Year, whenever.

DAVID S. BLANCHARD

GETTING THE DRIFT OF WINTER

No one lives in Syracuse, New York, for long without finding some way to make peace with winter. Snow is what we manufacture the most around here. It mixes with falling leaves early in November and dukes it out with the daffodils in April. I know what to expect, yet I am never ready.

When I woke to six inches the other day, I muttered about in search of gloves and a hat and scraper for the car before starting out to an early appointment. I was lost in thought about possible delays to a flight I was scheduled to take, the need for new tires, the urgency to get the storm windows in place, the leaves raked, and the garden mulched. All the standard winter worries. Then like a gong awakening me, a snow ball splashed against metal. I thought some kids had chosen my car as a handy target, but I soon saw that it was the stop sign that had been hit. I looked around to see the culprit. There he was, grinning broadly, rubbing his hands together in pride over his bulls-eye. A fellow about eighty years old. He waved. I waved. He smiled. I smiled.

I had a feeling he knew something about winter that I could stand to learn. By the time my appointment was over, most of the snow had melted. I had missed my chance to welcome winter. With a little practice, I'll have learned something by April.

DAVID S. BLANCHARD

KALEIDOSCOPE

KALEIDOSCOPE

Through a kaleidoscope the world becomes fractured, divided twenty-four ways in symmetrical pieces. A single candle flame becomes twenty-four flickering candles, each a perfect replica of the other. The mundane is made exquisite when it is placed in a pattern of identical squares; the ordinary becomes the mystical when it is seen through a prism.

Is this how life is, if only we step back far enough to see it all—a kaleidoscope of events joining, merging, dancing in rhythmic harmony? Could we appreciate the order of life, if we were not one of the fragments? But we are in it, of it, not observers of the pattern but part of the very texture of which it is constructed.

There may be a plan, but we will never be able to stand back far enough to appreciate it. Somewhere life may make sense to a great cosmic someone, but not to us here; not to us, splintered in a struggle to do what is right in a world that presents us with complex, competing options. We may never see the larger picture, creation's perfected whole; we may be forever flickering fragments, fractured by the raw reality of immediacy from which there is no escape while we are alive.

Well then, let us dance in the flame that we see.
Let the arc of our creativity embrace our moments
of time, and let us add our light to the kaleidoscope,
trusting in the unity of the whole even as we seek
symmetry with the part.

ELIZABETH TARBOX

BETWEEN NIGHT AND DAY

We must learn to reawaken and keep ourselves
awake, not by mechanical aids, but by an infinite
expectation of the dawn.

—HENRY DAVID THOREAU, *WALDEN*

Thoreau recognized a special power in the image of
the dawn, which "contains an earlier, more sacred
and auroral hour" and an invitation to awaken to "a
poetic or divine life." In its not-asleep-yet-not-quite-
awake quality, the dawn suspended him in a spirit of
awakening and regeneration.

How few mornings do I experience dawn's
awakening. Instead of a mechanical device, the cold
nose of an impatient dog interrupts my sleep. Then
the "Today Show" announces the news and weather
and the daily routine begins. Occasionally when I
get out for an early jog, I do awaken to the power of

dawn. The air is still; a layer of steam rolls over the glassy water of a nearby lake; congregations of geese chatter in a mystical cacophony. The sky is shaded with subtle pinks and blues—lovely, but not spectacular—and sometimes a star or a sliver of moon lingers from the night.

If I try to name the special power of dawn, I come up with words like stillness, silence, creativity, possibility, renewal. When the day awakes and we awaken, we move through a fuzzy transitional time. We may not be certain where we are or what day it is—we are suspended in time and space. If we awaken naturally, as Thoreau urges, we are conscious of having been in another world—in our dreaming selves. Thoreau calls this other world the "infinite mind." Dawn, he says, is a time when the will is still asleep and "the mind works like a machine without friction."

Somewhere between night and day there is a time—a consciousness—when we can look at the sun and the moon and the stars all at once and connect with "an earlier, more sacred and auroral hour." Dawn is sacred time. Usually we sleep through it.

SARAH YORK

BETWEEN DAY AND NIGHT

I went at sundown to the top of Dr. Ripley's hill and renewed my vows to the Genius of that place. Somewhat of awe, somewhat grand and solemn mingles with the beauty that shines afar around. In the West, where the sun was sinking behind the clouds, one pit of splendour lay as in a desert of space—a deposit of still light, not radiant.

—RALPH WALDO EMERSON, *JOURNAL*

One fall evening I went for a walk along a New England country path that opened onto a meadow, then wound along the edge of a lake, into the woods, and through rolling hills and farms. It was dusk and I bathed in the silence and stillness of the hour. The lake, though steamy in the morning, now reflected the golden trees, the falling leaves, and the changing colors of sunset. I paused to consider how the mood was different from the mood of dawn. The words that came to mind were "silence" and "stillness"—but a different stillness than that of the dawn. This was a stillness of peace, calm, enchantment, and mystery. I understood Emerson when he says, "Yet sweet and native as all those fair impressions on that summit fall on the eye and ear, they are not yet mine."

Between day and night we can look at the sun and the moon and the stars together, just as we can between night and day. At dusk, however, we are more conscious of being what Emerson calls "a stranger in nature." Dawn is our time of promise and self-reliance; dusk reminds us that for all of our knowledge of light and dark, we live in mystery.

SARAH YORK

CALM SOUL

The calm soul of all things calls to me from the place where the ocean meets the land. I see creation misted over the gentle water, moving along the snow-flecked shore.

I hear creation from the throat of the sea gull and the crow. I see God in the light-bright extravagance of sunrise and the movement of buffleheads rearranging their feathers and watching for the warmth, and I hear God in the gently falling clumps of snow as the winter-wrapped trees give up their gloves for spring.

God crashes over frozen rocks spraying ideas above my head, glinting with morning, too fleeting to catch. God plays at my feet, nudging and hinting and inviting my participation. God is restless and free, moving to the call of the wind. God is that moment when I lose myself to something which is beyond and within me. And somewhere, along the soft edges of the morning, it comes to me that God is a feeling prompted by love.

ELIZABETH TARBOX

(Inspired by "Calm Soul of All Things" by Matthew Arnold, in Hymns for the Celebration of Life, *Unitarian Universalist Association, Boston.)*

WITH EYES WIDE OPEN

If you've ever had a CAT scan, that computerized series of fancy X-rays, you know what it's like. You're alone in a totally white high-tech room in a hospital, lying on your back, arms above your head, instructed to stay stock-still for forty-five minutes or so. The table you're on slowly moves into or through a machine that is round and white and smooth and sleek. The scanner surrounds you. There is no one to talk to. The room is still. There is nothing in your fixed line of vision except the uninterrupted surface of the CAT scanner. You see nothing at all, really, until your eye catches four or five holes, apertures of varying sizes, a few inches from your face. And around these holes, around the only points your immobilized gaze might focus its attention, is written, "Danger, laser activity, do not look at these holes!"

I'm always really sorry that I noticed those holes in the first place. It would have been so much easier not to have seen them, to believe the scanner was an unblemished surface unworthy of particular focus. Now that I know the apertures are there, I have to close my eyes.

In life outside the scanner, on the other hand, we can live with eyes wide open. An aperture comes into view—a concentrated window onto the cosmos at large, the mysteries of human nature, one person's soul, the perplexities of existence—and we can focus our eyes on the power. To be able to open our eyes to the immensity is one of our great blessings.

JANE RANNEY RZEPKA

CLOSED FOR BUSINESS

The sign on the door said "Closed for Business," yet the images in my memory were very much open and alive.

The Westcott Variety Store had gone out of business. For decades it was an institution in that little business district just east of the university. Now it had gone the way of jacks, penny candy, and the hula hoop, although it's a safe bet that those items were still in stock on the day the store closed. The

Westcott Variety store had everything you needed, and a good number of things you couldn't ever possibly imagine needing, jammed into narrow aisles.

Now it was empty, barren. I stood at the window, looking in. What I saw was more than my reflection; I saw a good deal of my past.

I would guess my memories of that place are "preconscious." During my first year of life we lived just a few blocks away, and my mother tells of dragging me and my brother on a sled to the store on errands. As I grew up, the Westcott Variety Store was the place we went each year to pick out characters and creatures to augment the featured players in our family crèche. They are not very beautiful, at least to my adult aesthetic sense, but they were the greatest thing to a child.

The Westcott Variety Store was the kind of place a kid could go with a meager allowance and feel wealthy. It was a good place to buy a present for your grandmother. The search for birthday party favors began and ended in the bins by the front counter, divided by glass, full of marvelous trinkets.

It was July when we moved back to Syracuse a few years ago. I wanted window boxes, but all the garden supply stores were out of stock. In a moment of inspiration, I knew who to call. Not only did the Westcott Variety Store have window boxes, they had a choice of sizes and colors as well. It has been said, and it may be true, that it was impossible *not* to find what you wanted there.

The Westcott Variety Store remained the antithesis of the modern store to its closing day. Perhaps that is why it couldn't last. One does not get rich selling corncob pipes, mouse traps, and wooden clothespins. So, like a lot of things we have come to let go of, we realize that we have been enriched for a time by people and places that must eventually live only in the realm of memory. It is a worthy reminder to take a close look at those things we treasure while we still have the chance. It won't make them last any longer. But it can give them the permanence that lets them be seen in the reflection of a plate glass window of an empty store by a busy street on a summer day.

DAVID S. BLANCHARD

TAKE A LETTER

"I'm sorry to be writing you such a long letter. I didn't have time to write a short one."
—E. B. WHITE, IN A LETTER TO A FRIEND

I'm one of the last of the great letter writers. People frequently tell me what a wonderful correspondent I am. This usually from people who never write back, but pick up the phone on occasion. Yet I keep writing in the hopes that someone other than Ed McMahon will write.

The technology of phone calls and letters determines the sort of expression that they are best at delivering. Phone calls are transmitted. The voice is broken down into a scattering of signals, and then reassembled as other words flow past us. Letters, written words, by their nature are solid. Letters are slow and plodding. They clutter up desks. They are stories where phone calls are signals. We live by both, even if we have gotten a lot more accustomed to just sending out signals into the void, rather than struggling to narrate what it means to look into the void, to be faithful to the human predicament, to occupy the silences with the voice of our imagination.

The silences of phone calls are quickly filled; they can seem almost dangerous. But the silences of a letter can be fertile and nurturing. Some of those silences come from the writer, as an idea struggled with, and some are created by the readers who can proceed at their own speed into the new territory unfolded before them.

Long or short, letters are invitations into the interior of life in a way that a phone call can rarely match. I suppose I keep writing as a means of understanding where I have been and where I am

going. When I add "please write" to a letter, I really
mean it. If time is short, a long letter would be fine.

DAVID S. BLANCHARD

THE WISDOM TO KNOW THE DIFFERENCE

My colleague Harry Meserve described as a pleasant
surprise of advancing years the discovery of areas of
knowledge, activity, and enjoyment that he had
never before had time for or even considered. "This
discovery," he writes, "reminds one that no matter
how distinguished, competent, and successful we
may have been . . . we are now as little children who
must be taught from the start how to make our way
in other fields of knowledge and activity. Such
experience is good for the soul."

Aging is a lifelong process of adjustment to
change. The people who age best are those who are
granted serenity—as the famous prayer puts it—the
serenity to accept the things they cannot change, the
courage to change the things they can, and the
wisdom to know the difference.

Getting older is one of those things that cannot
be changed. The losses are different for different
people. Sometimes the loss means giving up posses-
sions to move into a smaller home, or giving up

independence to move in with a family member. Or it may be the loss of physical abilities—hearing, walking, seeing. Gradually, age reminds us that we can't do things we used to do. Age forces us to redefine ourselves in terms of what we can do. It is an art to be able to grow through the losses and accept the process without giving in to a spirit of decline.

Aging is a process of growth, not of decline. I admire people who age well more than those who remain youthful. Sometimes it is hard to tell the difference, for both may appear vital and alert. But one avoids the realities of the autumn season of life by pretending that it's still summer, while the other enjoys the brilliant colors.

SARAH YORK

LOVE CONTEST

My husband called from England. "I miss you," he said.

"I miss you, too," I answered.

"But I miss you more than you miss me," he said.

"No," I came back, "I think I miss you more."

"But you're at home, with the church and friends," he said, "and I'm in a strange hotel. I miss you more."

"No," I argued, "I'm here at home with all the responsibility for the kids and the laundry and the housecleaning. . . . I miss you more."

And so we argued, each of us defining our missing in terms of our own need, until we decided that only the telephone company would benefit from our little love contest.

In more recent years I have realized that we sometimes don't really miss each other and may feel guilty about it, while other times we do miss each other and still need to be apart. Most importantly, missing isn't always connected with physical presence. We can be absent while we are together or together while we are absent. We need to be together. We need to be apart. Our separate needs do not always coincide.

Once when I was in the mountains for some time apart, I sat on the porch reflecting upon the human needs for individual growth and relationship. At the same time I noticed some things in the front yard. The wisteria I had cut back the previous year was winding its way up a dogwood tree. The grapevines on the fence were thoroughly entwined in a climbing rosebush. On another part of the fence the honeysuckle was thriving—triumphant, even, over the poison ivy. A large bittersweet bush wound its tentacles around an old apple tree.

As I planned an evening of pruning, I made a few connections. Vines have a hard time living with other plants: They cling, they choke, they pursue their own growth. They compete with each other. Properly pruned, they can live and let live.

When we act like vines, we need to be pruned. But we get in trouble when we try to prune each other. What we need is a self-pruning mechanism, to check the urge to cling to or choke or dominate other life. If someone else tries to prune our needs and desires, it just doesn't work. If we can prune them for ourselves, then we understand better how the growth we cut back now yields a healthier relationship in the long run.

SARAH YORK

PROMISES, PROMISES

There is a fellow who shares my surname, yet with whom I have no relation, who has made a fortune writing books that are pitched as guides to success in any number of fields. It all started with the volume entitled "The One-Minute Manager." It's been a bestseller and has spawned several sequels that have made the other Mr. Blanchard a millionaire. I've been contemplating a book called, "The One-Minute Marriage," not to describe failed relationships, but offering a nifty program to marital bliss through sixty-second solutions. I know there is a market, but I have only been able to think of one thing that could be confined to the current cultural attention span of a minute. Just one, and that's if I talk fast.

There are some weighty obstacles. For one, in a marriage, unlike the world of business and management, you cannot delegate the hard work. You have to do it yourselves. And second, the key elements to happiness in any relationship are always changing. Today we need a great sense of humor. Tomorrow what's required is forgiveness. The day after that, maybe a spirit of playfulness. And on and on. At weddings I often feel couples expect me to offer some sage advice that will enrich their marriage. The fact is, I haven't a clue what it is they'll need. Most of the time I'm not so sure what I need in my most intimate relationships.

I often leave my counsel to this: Do more than simply keep the promises made in your vows. Do something more: keep promising. As time passes, keep promising new things, deeper things, vaster things, yet-unimagined things. Promises that will be needed to fill the expanses of time and of love. To keep promising, you won't need a license, you won't need witnesses, you won't need a minister. You will only need what you already have: each other.

Keep promising . . .

DAVID S. BLANCHARD

ABOUT THE AUTHORS

David S. Blanchard has been the minister to the First Unitarian Universalist Society of Syracuse, New York, since 1989. Prior to that he served a congregation in Lexington, Kentucky. Blanchard is a graduate of St. Lawrence University and Harvard Divinity School. He shares his household with his partner, two teen-aged daughters, and a stray dog that stayed.

Jane Ranney Rzepka grew up a Unitarian in Ohio. After graduating from Starr King School for the Ministry, she earned a doctorate from the Graduate Theological Union and the University of California, Berkeley. She is the co-author of the preaching textbook *Thematic Preaching* and served a Unitarian Universalist congregation in Reading, Massachusetts, for fifteen years before moving to the Church of the Larger Fellowship in Boston. Rzepka has trekked in Nepal with her family, camped off-road with her mother in the Sahara, and traveled on the Amazon.

Elizabeth Tarbox died in 1999. For two years before her death she served as the minister at First Parish in Cohasset, Massachusetts. She is the author of another meditation manual, *Evening Tide.*

Sarah York is a Unitarian Universalist minister who has served congregations in New York, Maryland, California, and England. York is also the author of *Remembering Well: Rituals for Celebrating Life and Mourning Death, The Holy Intimacy of Strangers,* and *Pilgrim Heart: The Inner Journey Home.* She lives on a farm in North Carolina with her husband Chuck, where she grows herbs, flowers, and vegetables, and enjoys creating ways to share the harvest with others.

ALSO FROM SKINNER HOUSE BOOKS

Day of Promise: Collected Meditations, Volume One.
Collected by Kathleen Montgomery.
An anthology of one hundred meditations from more
than forty authors. ISBN 1-55896-419-3.

What We Share: Collected Meditations, Volume Two.
Collected by Patricia Frevert.
Meditations from Richard S. Gilbert, Bruce T. Marshall,
Elizabeth Tarbox, and Lynn Ungar. ISBN 1-55896-423-1.

All the Gifts of Life: Collected Meditations, Volume Three.
Collected by Patricia Frevert.
Meditations from Robert R. Walsh, Barbara Rohde, Gary
A. Kowalski, and Meg Barnhouse. ISBN 1-55896-437-1.

Singing in the Night: Collected Meditations, Volume Five.
Collected by Mary Benard.
Meditations from Jane Ellen Mauldin, David O. Rankin,
Gordon B. McKeeman, and Kaaren Solveig Anderson.
Available Fall 2003. ISBN 1-55896-444-4.